What Christians Should Know About...

The Glory of God

Ed Roebert

Sovereign World

ISBN: 1 85240 234 2

This Sovereign World book is distributed in North America by
Renew Books, a ministry of Gospel Light, Ventura, California, USA.
For a free catalog of resources from Renew Books/Gospel Light,
please contact your Christian supplier or call 1-800-4-GOSPEL.

SOVEREIGN WORLD LIMITED
P.O. Box 777, Tonbridge, Kent TN11 0ZS, England.

Typeset and printed in the UK by Sussex Litho Ltd, Chichester, West Sussex.

Contents

About the Author

Pastor Ed, as he was so fondly known, was the Senior Pastor of the Hatfield Christian Church in Pretoria South Africa, where he faithfully served the Lord for over thirty four years. He and his wife Pal played a major role in the Charismatic Movement in South Africa in the late sixties and seventies, and as a result the Church at Hatfield grew from a small church to a mega church and soon became the largest in Pretoria.

Pastor Ed always had a longing for revival and loved to see the Holy Spirit at work, changing people's lives. He was completely open to the new move of God, also known as the Toronto Blessing, and he encouraged his people to keep going deeper into the River. As he led the people into God's presence, he would invite the Holy Spirit to come and then allow Him time to do whatever He wanted to do. He referred to this as 'hanging in'. Many a time the glory of God would come down and God's presence would be almost tangible.

In his last sermon entitled **The Glory of God** he mentioned that it is the easiest thing for a preacher to fill the sixty or hundred and twenty-minute church service with all sorts of programming. It's the most difficult thing to back off and let the Holy Spirit have a shot. "Sometimes it takes me out of my comfort zone," he said, "but I have made a decision to say Yes! to the Holy Spirit. I've seen incredible things happen at such times. I've seen people absolutely pent up with problems and someone prays for them and as they fall to the floor and lie there for half-an-hour, one hour, two hours, three hours, they get up totally transformed. Something that would have taken endless counselling, is done within moments as the Spirit of God falls upon them." He often said, " Don't be afraid of the Holy Spirit, He will never do you any harm."

In July 1997, at the age of 57, Pastor Ed died of heart failure at the beginning of a big 'March for the Nations' which marked the conclusion of the Global Cosultation on World Evangelisation (GCOWE) Conference which was held at the Hatfield Christian Church in Pretoria, where close to 130 nations were represented.

His wife Pal, and three sons Andrew, Peter and John are all part of the ongoing ministry at Hatfield.

Introduction

For a long time I've been intrigued and fascinated by the subject of the glory of the Lord. I've often broached the subject and wanted to share on it, but because it seemed to refer to so many things I could not put together, I would get confused and I would back off from sharing about it. But I feel that I've come to the stage in my life where I can speak about the glory of the Lord. As we study this subject, we are going to attempt to answer the question, What is the Glory of God? and then see how God's glory can touch our lives personally.

Part 1   What is the Glory of God?

In an attempt to answer this question we are going to look at five answers.

Part 2   Lord Show Me Your Glory

Part 1

What is the Glory of God?

1.1 God's Presence

God's glory is experienced in His presence! If we want to experience the glory of God, it will come through experiencing the presence of the Lord as a reality in our lives. It is in His presence that our spiritual senses are quickened, and we become more aware of the spiritual realm.

When Jesus drew near to the two men on the road to Emmaus, they said to each other that their hearts had burned inside them, when Jesus had talked to them. In other words, their spiritual senses were quickened by God's presence and they had actually experienced the glory of God. As we experience the reality of the presence of the Lord, we too will experience His glory.

In first Samuel chapter four, we read of God's glory and His presence being closely associated, although with negative ramifications. Eli had died, his sons had been killed and the ark of the covenant had been captured. The **ark of the covenant** spoke clearly of the **presence of God**. Over the ark of the covenant were the two cherubim and on the lid of the ark of the covenant was the mercy seat. It was on the mercy seat that the Shekinah glory (the supernatural light or cloud) rested, which was the symbol of God's presence.

> *Then she (Eli's daughter-in-law) named the child Ichabod, saying, "The glory has departed from Israel!" because the ark of God had been captured... And she said, "The glory has departed from Israel, for the ark of God has been captured."* (1 Samuel 4:21,22)

The ark of God which was the symbol of the presence of God, had been captured and was gone, so Eli's daughter-in-law said:

"Ichabod, the glory has departed," the presence of God has gone. From this story we learn that without God's presence, there will be no glory!

I have heard of a certain church that knew and experienced the power and the presence of God, but sin came into the church and the church became cold and rational. The story goes on to say that somebody wrote across the wall of the church 'Ichabod'. The glory has departed!

I myself could not remain in a situation where God's presence had departed. I've got to be where God is. I've got to be at a place where I can experience the presence of God. If you do not experience the presence of God personally, may I encourage you to press into the presence of God until you touch Him. The presence of God is more important than bread and butter. It is more important than the clothes that you wear. If all of a sudden, while you are worshipping God, an awesome sense of the presence of God comes upon you, you can legitimately say that you have tasted God's glory.

I am of the opinion that God wants to show His glory in many churches. He wants to ultimately demonstrate His presence and His glory across the world.

> *But truly, as I live, all the earth shall be filled with the* **glory** *of the Lord.* (Numbers 14:21)

The day is coming soon when the glory of the Lord will cover the earth as the waters cover the sea, and we are privileged to see the beginnings of that take place.

Let me ask you a question! Is the presence of God a reality to you, or have you lost the sense of God's presence in your own life? If God's presence is not a reality to you, you need to take time to become still before God and ask the Holy Spirit to make God's presence real to you. Wait in His presence and with the eyes of your heart see Jesus looking at you. Keep looking at Him and just silently sit in His presence. This does not come easily to our natural mind, but as you keep on practising entering into God's presence, in time, it will become easier.

Most people long for God's presence and unfortunately in

many places where God's presence is supposed to be felt, it is not felt. People go to church in order to meet with God, but often they never meet Him. Jesus wants to come and manifest Himself to us individually so that we may personally experience the glory of His presence.

> *He who has My commandments and keeps them, he it is who loves Me. And he who loves Me will be loved by My Father, and I will love him and **manifest Myself** to him.* (John 14:21)

If we do not give God time to manifest His presence to us but press ahead with our own agendas, we limit God. Pastors find it easy to fill a church service with all sorts of programmes, but they feel out of their comfort zone, when it comes to stopping what they are doing and inviting the Holy Spirit to take over. Waiting for God's presence to be manifested is the hardest thing to do, but if we long to see God's glory, we must learn to press into His presence.

1.2 God's Greatness

In the scriptures we notice that the glory of God and His greatness often go hand in hand. Therefore if we want to see God's glory, we need to take a look at His greatness.

> *Surely, the Lord our God has shown us His **glory** and **His greatness**, and we have heard His voice from the midst of the fire. We have seen this day that God speaks with man; yet he still lives.* (Deuteronomy 5:24)

God's Greatness at Mount Sinai

Look at Mount Sinai for a moment. The people are gathered around the mountain and suddenly a cloud comes down over it and there's lightning and the rumble of thunder. The mountain trembles at the presence of God and the sound of a trumpet is heard that resounds across the entire camp of the Israelites. The children of Israel look up at the mountain and they know that God has arrived in His greatness and His glory.

> *Then the Lord said to Moses, "Go to the people and sanctify them today and tomorrow, and let them wash their clothes. And let them be ready for the third day. For on the third day the Lord will come down upon Mount Sinai in the sight of all the people." You shall set bounds for the people all around saying. "Take heed to yourselves that you do not go up to the mountain or touch its base. Whoever touches the mountain shall surely be put to death."* (Exodus 19:10-12)

> *And Moses brought the people out of the camp to meet with God, and they stood at the foot of the mountain. Now Mount Sinai was completely in smoke, because the Lord descended upon it in fire.*
> *It's smoke ascended like the smoke of a furnace and the whole mountain quaked.* (Exodus 19:17,18)

What an awesome experience this was for the children of Israel, as God visually demonstrated His greatness to them and in doing so, He showed them His glory!

There's something in everyone of us that says, "God is great, Great is the Lord". That is why that song became a favourite when it was penned some years ago; "Then sings my soul my Saviour God to Thee, How great Thou art! How great Thou art!"

God's Greatness in the Psalms

David had a revelation of God's glory as displayed through His greatness.

> *The voice of the Lord is over the waters;* ***The God of glory thunders;*** *The Lord is over many waters. The voice of the Lord is powerful; The voice of the Lord is full of majesty. The voice of the Lord breaks the cedars, Yes the Lord splinters the cedars of Lebanon. He makes them also skip like a calf, Lebanon and Sirion like a young wild ox. The*

voice of the Lord divides the flames of fire. The voice of the Lord shakes the wilderness; The Lord shakes the wilderness of Kadesh. The voice of the Lord makes the deer give birth, and strips the forest bare; and in His temple everyone says ***Glory!*** (Psalm 29:3-9)

David also described God's greatness as being unsearchable.

Great is the Lord and highly to be praised, and His greatness is so vast and so deep as to be unsearchable.
(Psalm 145:3 Amplified)

Jeremiah had a revelation of God's greatness and could say that there was nothing too hard for God to do.

Alas, Lord God! Behold, You made the heavens and the earth by Your great power and by Your stretched out arm! There is nothing too hard or too wonderful for You.
(Jeremiah 32:17 Amplified)

We too need a divine revelation of God's greatness and His might, because when we see this we will be seeing His glory.

1.3 God's Signs, Wonders and Miracles

The glory of God also refers to God's signs, wonders and miracles that He performs.

*Because all these men who have seen **My glory** and the **signs** which I did in Egypt and in the wilderness, and have put Me to the test now these ten times, and have not heeded My voice. Surely they shall not see the land which I sware unto their fathers.* (Numbers 14:22)

After the children of Israel had passed through the Red sea, and all the Egyptians who were pursuing them lay dead on the sea shore, the Bible says that Israel saw the great work, the wonder that God had performed, and the fear of God fell upon them.

> *Thus Israel saw the great work (wonder) which the Lord had done in Egypt; so the people feared the Lord, and believed the Lord and His servant Moses.* (Exodus 14:31)

God's Signs in Egypt

> *So the Lord said to Moses: "See I have made you as God to Pharaoh, and Aaron your brother shall be your prophet. You shall speak all that I command you. And Aaron your brother shall speak to Pharoah, that he he must send the children of Israel out of his land. And I will harden Pharoah's heart, and multiply My **signs** and My **wonders** in the land of Egypt."* (Exodus 7:1-3)

The Ten Plagues

Each of the ten plagues were signs and wonders performed by God, that demonstrated His glory.

The water in the River Nile turned into blood.

> *Thus says the Lord, "By this you shall know that I am the Lord. Behold I will strike the waters which are in the river with the rod that is in my hand, and they shall be turned to blood."* (Exodus 7:17)

The entire land was smitten with a plague of frogs.

> *So Aaron stretched out his hand over the waters of Egypt and the frogs came up and covered the land of Egypt.* (Exodus 8 :6)

The dust of the land of Egypt became lice.

> *So the Lord said to Moses, "Say to Aaron, 'Stretch out your*

13

rod and strike the dust of the land, so that It may become lice throughout all the land of Egypt.'" (Exodus 8:16)

The land was filled with swarms of flies.

"If you will not let My people go, behold, I will send swarms of flies on you and your servants, on your people and into your houses. The houses of the Egyptians shall be full of swarms of flies, and also the ground on which they stand."
(Exodus 8:21)

A severe disease broke out on all the livestock of Egypt and all died.

"Behold, the hand of the Lord will be on your cattle in the field, on the horses, on the donkeys, on the camels, on the oxen and on the sheep. There will be a very severe pestilence." (Exodus 9:3)

Boils broke out in sores on both man and beast throughout Egypt.

So the Lord said to Moses and Aaron, "Take for yourselves handfuls of ashes from a furnace, and let Moses scatter it towards the heavens in the sight of Pharaoh. And it will become fine dust in all the land of Egypt, and it will cause boils that break out in sores on man and beast throughout all the land." (Exodus 9:8,9)

The Lord sent thunder and hail on the land of Egypt.

And the Lord sent thunder and hail, and fire darted to the ground. And the Lord rained hail on the land of Egypt. So there was hail, and fire mingled with the hail, so very heavy that there was none like it in all the land of Egypt since it became a nation. And the hail struck throughout the whole land of Egypt, all that was in the field, both man and beast; and the hail struck every herb of the field and broke every tree of the field. (Exodus 9:23-25)

A plague of locusts covered the face of the land.

> *"Or else if you refuse to let My people go, behold, tomorrow I will bring locusts into your territory. And they shall cover the face of the earth, so that no one will be able to see the earth, and they shall eat the residue of what is left, which remains from the hail, and they shall eat every tree which grows up for you out of the field. And they shall fill your houses, the houses of your servants, and the houses of all the Egyptians."* (Exodus 10:4-6)

Thick darkness covered the land of Egypt.

> *Then the Lord said to Moses, "Stretch out your hand toward heaven, that there may be darkness over the land of Egypt, darkness which may even be felt."* (Exodus 10:21)

All the firstborn in the land of Egypt died.

> *Then Moses said, "Thus says the Lord: About midnight I will go out into the midst of Egypt; And all the firstborn in the land of Egypt shall die, from the firstborn of Pharoah who sits on the throne, even to the firstborn of the maidservant who is behind the handmill, and all the firstborn of the beasts."* (Exodus 11:4,5)

All of these plagues were signs demonstrating God's glory and power.

The Sign in Cana of Galilee

In the second chapter of the gospel of John, the story is recorded of Jesus being present at the marriage feast in Cana of Galilee and of how He turned the water into wine. This sign that Jesus performed, was a manifestation of His glory. John writing about this story says,

> *This beginning of signs Jesus did in Cana of Galilee, and*

15

manifested His glory, and His disciples believed in Him.
(John 2:11)

The Glory of God Manifested Through Miracles

If a sick or maimed person comes to a church service, and prayer is offered for them and God gives them a new limb, or supernaturally heals them, that is a manifestation of the glory of God.

A young lady came to our church, having fallen in an ice-skating accident and they were afraid that she had broken her neck. They were scared to move her and they left her lying on the ice-rink for forty-five minutes. By the time the medics arrived she was just about frozen, and owing to the fact that she only had one kidney (the other having been previously removed) she picked up an infection in the remaining kidney and was in real trouble. Because of the infection the doctors had put her on a drip, and had placed a neck brace on her neck. In that condition, she came to church seeking prayer. A young man prayed for her and as he prayed for her healing, the power of God hit her and she fell over backwards. The neck brace supernaturally popped off and the drip in her arm was ripped out, nobody pulled it out but it ended up about three metres away from her. When she phoned the doctor the next day, he said that she could have actually died as a result of this because she could not have lived without the drip assisting her remaining kidney for more than two hours. The following week, when they took her in for X-rays, they found that a miracle had taken place and that a second kidney had appeared, and she was completely healed.

That is the glory of God, manifested through a miracle. Every time God performs a miracle, He displays His glory. Let's trust God for a greater demonstration of His glory through signs, wonders and miracles.

1.4 God's Goodness

God is a good God and whenever we experience His goodness,

we are also experiencing His glory. Moses asked God to show him His glory and God showed him His goodness.

God Showed Moses His Goodness and His Glory

> *And he (Moses) said, "Please, show me Your **glory**." Then God said, "I will make all My **goodness** pass before you, and I will proclaim the name of the Lord before you. I will be gracious to whom I will be gracious, and I will have compassion on whom I will have compassion."* (Exodus 33:18,19)

> *Then the Lord descended in the cloud and stood with him there, and proclaimed the name of the Lord. And the Lord passed before him and proclaimed, "The Lord, the Lord God, merciful and gracious, longsuffering and **abounding in goodness** and truth, keeping mercy for thousands, forgiving iniquity and transgression and sin, by no means clearing the guilty, visiting the iniquity of the fathers upon the children and the children's children to the third and the fourth generation."* (Exodus 34:5-7)

Having experienced God's goodness was such an awesome experience for Moses, that his automatic reaction was to bow his head and worship God.

> *So Moses made haste and bowed his head toward the earth and worshipped.* (Exodus 34:8)

When we begin to understand a little more of the glory of God as manifested through His goodness, we too will just want to fall down and worship God.

God's Goodness to the Children of Israel

In their journey through the wilderness, God displayed His goodness towards the Israelites every day, by supplying all their needs.

Marvelous things He did in the sight of their fathers... He divided the sea and caused them to pass through; And He made the waters stand up like a heap. In the daytime also He led them with a cloud, and all the night with a light of fire. He split the rocks in the wilderness, and gave them drink in abundance like the depths. He also brought streams out of the rock, and caused waters to run down like rivers.
(Psalm 78:12-16)

Yet He had commanded the clouds above, and opened the doors of heaven. Had rained down manna on them to eat, and given them of the bread of heaven. Men ate angel's food; He sent them food to the full.   (Psalm 78:23-25)

He also rained meat on them like the dust. Feathered fowl like the sand of the sea. And He let them fall in the midst of their camp, all around their habitations. So they ate and were well filled.   (Psalm 78:27-29)

Even although the Israelites were rebellious, God continued to show them His goodness, because it is part of His character. Through His goodness, God demonstrated His glory to them, but they failed to recognise it. Every time we experience God's goodness to us, we are experiencing His glory, but most times we are unaware of it.

May God quicken our spiritual senses to perceive His glory whenever we experience His goodness.

1.5 God's Judgements

The glory of God also refers to His judgements. In Ezekiel, chapter thirty-nine, we notice how the glory of God is aligned with the judgement of God.

*I will set My **glory** among the nations; all the nations shall see My **judgement** which I have executed and My hand which I have laid on them.*   (Ezekiel 39:21)

In this verse God says that He is going to show His glory through His judgements. As human beings, we naturally shy away from God's judgements, but here we notice that God's glory and God's judgement sometimes go hand in hand.

In the fourteenth chapter of Numbers we read of an awesome incident that took place in the lives of the children of Israel as they journeyed through the wilderness.

The Children of Israel Murmured

> *Then all the congregation lifted up their voices and cried, and the people wept that night. And all the children of Israel murmured against Moses and Aaron, and the whole congregation said to them, "If only we had died in the land of Egypt! Or if only we had died in this wilderness."*
> (Numbers 14:1,2)

The Israelites began to murmur and said: "We would rather have died in Egypt, we would rather have died in the wilderness." A frightening thing happened. God actually gave them their desire and they all died in the wilderness. I want to say descreetly yet gently. Do not open your big mouth and wish death upon yourself in given situations. You might get it! They said, "We wish we had died in the wilderness." God said, "You've got your wish."

They Wanted to Go Back to Egypt

> *"Why has the Lord brought us to this land to fall by the sword, that our wives and children should become victims? Would it not be better for us to return to Egypt?" So they said to one another, "Let us select a leader and return to Egypt."*
> (Numbers 14:3,4)

The Israelites wanted to go back to Egypt. Egypt speaks to us of the old life, of our old paradigms.There is always a desire for people to return to their old ways because change is not always comfortable but by God's grace we must determine to press on to greater heights because there is still much land to be possessed.

As I look back over the years that we have endeavoured to follow the Lord, it has been a wonderful experience and adventure for us. God has given us tremendous growth in many areas but some people have said, "Oh if only we could go back to the days in the little church!" Others said, "I wish we were back in the tent! I wish we were back in the days when the services were only one hour long." There are also those who said that they wished that they could come to church and not be stretched out of their comfort zones. Well the bad news is, that is not going to happen, because church was made for training soldiers. Church is boot camp!

The children of Israel said, "We wish we were back in Egypt, we would much rather be in the wilderness. We want the leeks, the onions and the garlic." Who wants leeks, onions and garlic, when you can have milk and honey?

The Israelites said, "Let's go back, let's look for a leader. Who's going to lead us back to Egypt?" Who wants to go back to a dead formalistic type of service, when you can have the move of God's Holy Spirit instead? Who wants to go back into dead orthodoxy, when you can come to church and sense the the glory of His presence? Who wants to go backward instead of forward?

The crux of the matter is that we cannot go back! God is taking us on into an exciting adventure with Him and we must determine to go forward with Him.

Recently God spoke to us as a church. He said that we are like people who have been swimming along in a river, and we have come to a waterfall and have gone over it. Once you've gone over a waterfall there's no going back. In terms of where God is taking us, we're going forward. There's no going back. If we do not have this kind of mentality, we are never going to make an impact for Christ on our generation.

> *Forgetting what lies behind and straining forward to what lies ahead, I press toward the goal to win the supreme and heavenly prize to which God in Christ Jesus is calling us upward.* (Philippians 3:13,14 Amplified)

The Glory of the Lord Appeared

The Israelites rebelled and murmured against Moses and Aaron and then Joshua and Caleb spoke to them and said:

> *"Only do not rebel against the Lord, nor fear the people of the land, for they are our bread; their protection has departed from them and the Lord is with us. Do not fear them." And all the congregation said to stone them with stones. Now the* **glory of the Lord appeared** *in the tabernacle of meeting before all the children of Israel. And the Lord said to Moses,"How long will these people reject Me? And how long will they not believe Me, with all the signs which I have performed among them?"* (Numbers 14:9-11)

Picture this scene! There is rebellion in the camp when all of a sudden in the height of their rebellion, the glory of God appears before their eyes, perhaps in the form of a supernatural light or a cloud, above the tabernacle of meeting. What an incredible sight that must have been!

God's Judgement

God's decision of judgement was clear and awesome. God appeared in the tabernacle and said to Moses:

> *"I will strike them with the pestilence and disinherit them, and I will make of you* (Joshua and Caleb) *a nation greater and mightier than they."* (Numbers 14:12)

God had had enough of these people, and He determined to wipe them out with pestilence and disinherit them, but to Joshua and Caleb He said that He would raise up from out of them, a new nation.

The Incredible Power of Intercession

> *And Moses said to the Lord, "Then the Egyptians will hear*

21

*it, for by Your might You brought these people up from them. And they will tell it to the inhabitants of this land. They have heard that You LORD are among these people; that You LORD are seen face to face and that Your cloud stands above them; and You go before them in a pillar of cloud by day and in a pillar of fire by night. Now if You kill these people as one man, then the nations which have heard of Your fame will speak saying, because the LORD was not able to bring this people to the land which He swore to give them therefore He killed them in the wilderness. And now, I pray, let the power of my LORD be great, just as You have spoken saying, The LORD is longsuffering and abundant in mercy, forgiving iniquity and transgression; but He by no means clears the guilty, visiting the iniquity of the fathers on the children to the third and forth generation. **Pardon the iniquity of this people I pray,** according to the greatness of Your mercy, just as You have forgiven this people, from Egypt even until now." Then the LORD said, "**I have pardoned** according to your word."* (Numbers 14:13-20)

From this incident we learn of the importance of intercession. Because there was an intercessor, God forgave their sin.

He will even deliver the one for whom you intercede, who is not innocent; yes, he will be delivered though the cleanness of your hands. (Job 22:30 Amplified)

God is longsuffering and loving and He does not want to just wipe people out. However, if they continue in their own wilful ways, God has to deal with their sin.

The Importance of Obeying God

*"Because all these men who have seen **My glory** and the signs which I did in Egypt and in the wilderness, and have put Me to the test now these ten times, and have **not heeded My voice**, they certainly shall not see the land of which I*

swore to their fathers, nor shall any of those who rejected Me see it. But My servant Caleb, because he has a different spirit in him and has followed Me fully, I will bring into the land where he went, and his descendants shall inherit it."

(Numbers 14:22-24)

Only those who obeyed God's voice had the privilege of entering into the promised land.

A Different Spirit

God desires to manifest His glory, but He wants to reveal His glory through people who have a different spirit. Instead of grumbling and complaining to God, they follow after Him and His ways with all their hearts. Because Joshua and Caleb had a different spirit and **followed God fully**, God brought them into the promised land.

God Gave the Children of Israel What They Asked for

*Then the LORD spoke to Moses and Aaron, saying, "How long shall I bear with this evil congregation who murmur against Me? I have heard the murmurings which the children of Israel murmur against Me. Say to them, As I live, says the LORD, just as you have spoken in My hearing, so I will do to you: The carcasses of you who have murmured against Me shall fall in this wilderness, all of you who were numbered, according to your entire number, from twenty years old and above. **Except for Caleb** the son of Jephunneh **and Joshua** the son of Nun, you shall by no means enter the land which I swore I would make you dwell in. But your little ones, whom you said would be victims, I will bring in, and they shall know the land which you have despised. But as for you, your carcasses shall fall in this wilderness. And your sons shall be shepherds in the wilderness forty years, and bear the brunt of your infidelity, until your carcasses are consumed in the wilderness. According to the number of the days in which*

23

you spied out the land, forty days, for each day you shall bear your guilt one year, namely forty years, and you shall know My rejection."   (Numbers 14:26-34)

In this story God's glory was portrayed in His judgement on those who wanted to go backwards instead of forward, and who rebelled against God's ways. Let us be people with a different spirit, who choose to put God first in our lives, and follow Him with all of our heart.

God's Judgement on Korah

Another illustration of the glory of God coming down on judgement on the children of Israel, is recorded in the story of Korah.

Now Korah the son of Izhar, the son of Kohath, the son of Levi, with Dathan and Abiram the sons of Eliab, and On the son of Peleth, sons of Reuben, took men; And they rose up before Moses with some of the children of Israel, two hundred and fifty leaders of the congregation, representatives of the congregation, men of renown.
                                                    (Numbers 16:1,2)

Their Conspiracy

Korah and his following of men, were envious of Moses and Aaron's position of leadership of the children of Israel and they conspired together and brought false accusations against them by suggesting that Moses and Aaron were exalting themselves above all the people and thought they were smarter than the rest of them. In doing so, Korah and his men were actually rebelling against God's appointed leadership.

They gathered together against Moses and Aaron, and said to them, "You take too much upon yourselves, for all the congregation is holy, every one of them, and the LORD is among them. Why then do you exalt yourselves above the congregation of the LORD?" (Numbers 16:3)

The Reaction of Moses

So when Moses heard it, he fell on his face; And he spoke to Korah and all his company, saying, "Tomorrow morning the LORD will show who is His and who is holy, and will cause him to come near to Him; that one whom He chooses He will cause to come near to Him. Do this: Take censers, Korah and all your company; Put fire in them and put incense in them before the LORD tomorrow, and it shall be that the man whom the LORD chooses shall be the holy one. You take too much upon yourselves, you sons of Levi!" Then Moses said to Korah, "Hear now, you sons of Levi: Is it a small thing to you that the God of Israel has separated you from the congregation of Israel, to bring you near to Himself, to do the work of the tabernacle of the LORD, and to stand before the congregation to serve them; And that He has brought you near to Himself, you and all your brethren, the sons of Levi, with you? And are you seeking the priesthood also? Therefore you and all your company are gathered together against the LORD. And what is Aaron that you murmur against him?" (Numbers 16:4-11)

The Stubbornness of Dathan and Abiram

Moses requested to see Dathan and Abiram, but they refused to come.

And Moses sent to call Dathan and Abiram the sons of Eliab, but they said, "We will not come up! Is it a small thing that you have brought us up out of a land flowing with milk and honey, to kill us in the wilderness, that you should keep acting like a prince over us? Moreover you have not brought us into a land flowing with milk and honey, nor given us inheritance of fields and vineyards. Will you put out the eyes of these men? We will not come up!" Then Moses was very angry, and said to the LORD, "Do not respect their offering. I have not taken one donkey from them, nor have I hurt one of them." (Numbers 16:12-15)

Moses' God-Given Strategy

And Moses said to Korah, "Tomorrow, you and all your company be present before the LORD, you and they, as well as Aaron. Each of you take his censer and put incense in it, and each of you bring his censer before the LORD, two hundred and fifty censers; you also, and Aaron, each of you with his censer." So every man took his censer, put fire in it, laid incense on it, and stood at the door of the tabernacle of meeting with Moses and Aaron. And Korah gathered all the congregation against them at the door of the tabernacle of meeting. **Then the glory of the LORD appeared to all the congregation.** *And the Lord spoke to Moses and Aaron, saying, "Separate yourselves from among this congregation, that I may consume them in a moment." Then they fell on their faces, and said, "O God, the God of the spirits of all flesh, shall one man sin, and You be angry with all the congregation?" So the LORD spoke to Moses, saying, "Speak to the congregation, saying, 'Get away from the tents of Korah, Dathan, and Abiram.' " Then Moses rose and went to Dathan and Abiram, and the elders of Israel followed him. And he spoke to the congregation, saying, "Depart now from the tents of these wicked men! Touch nothing of theirs, lest you be consumed in all their sins." So they got away from around the tents of Korah, Dathan, and Abiram; and Dathan and Abiram came out and stood at the door of their tents, with their wives, their sons, and their little children. Then Moses said, "By this you shall know that the LORD has sent me to do all these works, for I have not done them of my own will. If these men die naturally like all men, or if they are visited by the common fate of all men, then the LORD has not sent me. But if the LORD creates a new thing, and the earth opens its mouth and swallows them up with all that* *belongs to them, and they go down alive into the pit, then you will understand that these men have rejected the LORD."* (Numbers 16:16-30)

God's Judgement on Korah and His Men

Then it came to pass, as he finished speaking all these words, that the ground split apart under them, and the earth opened its mouth and swallowed them up, with their households and all the men with Korah, with all their goods. So they and all those with them went down alive into the pit; the earth closed over them, and they perished from among the congregation. Then all Israel who were around them fled at their cry, for they said, "Lest the earth swallow us up also!" And a fire came out from the LORD and consumed the two hundred and fifty men who were offering incense.

(Numbers 16:31-35)

The Glory of the Lord Appeared

*On the next day all the congregation of the children of Israel murmured against Moses and Aaron, saying, "You have killed the people of the LORD." Now it happened, when the congregation had gathered against Moses and Aaron, that they turned toward the tabernacle of meeting; and suddenly the cloud covered it, and **the glory of the LORD appeared.***

(Numbers 16:41-42)

What an awesome story of God's glory being seen in His judgement. Moses obviously had a very close relationship with God, and God revealed some of the intimate secrets of His heart to him. God must have somehow told Moses in his spirit what was going to happen to Korah and his followers, and by faith Moses spoke out the possiblity of their doom before it happened. As a sign that God had allowed His judgement to fall on Korah and his followers, the glory of the Lord appeared at the tent of

27

meeting. This must have bolstered Moses' faith!

Conclusion

This story comes to us as a warning not to play the fool with God, but to take Him seriously. The Bible reminds us that the time has come for judgement to begin in the house of God.

> *For the time has come for judgment to begin at the house of God; and if it begin with us first, what will be the end of those who do not obey the gospel of God?*　　(1 Peter 4:17)

Perhaps you are bound with the grave-clothes of tradition. Let God rip them off! Don't mess with Him when He does it! Don't interfere with the processes of God in your life! Respond to God! I urge you to let God change you. Let God take you forward. Tell God that whatever He has for you, you want it because you're going on with Him. Don't be like those who dig their heels in the ground and say to God, "So far and no further!" If that is your attitude, you will never experience God's glory. Rather have the attitude that says, "God I will follow You until the very end." When you feel like backing off a little, hear God say, "Son, daughter, another step forward." Make a decision never to get rigid or too old for what God is doing, and make up your mind to go all the way with God. May God help us never to draw back, but to keep on following after His plan and destiny for our lives.

Instead of the glory of God falling upon us in judgement, let us allow the glory of God to fall upon us in the blessings of **His presence, His greatness, His signs wonders and miracles,** and **His goodness.**

Part 2

Lord Show Me Your Glory

2.1 The Prayer of Moses

Many people have heard about the glory of God, but few have specifically asked God to show them His glory. The Bible says in James 4:2 that we have not because we ask not. Moses asked God to show him His glory.

> *And Moses said, "I beseech You, show me Your glory."*
> (Exodus 33:18)

Shortly after Moses had placed this request before God, God honoured his request and gave him a revelation of His glory. For many of us who have made a similar request to God, the time has come for a break-through into experiencing the reality of God's glory.

Preparing Ourselves for a Revelation of His Glory

God said to Moses, "You have asked Me to show you My glory, but I want you to get ready and prepare yourself and come up the mountain in the morning and present yourself to Me."

> *"Be ready and come up in the morning to Mount Sinai, and present yourself there to Me on the top of the mountain."*
> (Exodus 34:2)

Just like Moses, we need to prepare ourselves for a revelation of God's glory. In preparing ourselves it is important that we must have dealt with sin in our lives. If we are aware of anything that is wrong, we need to put it right. Sin can block us off from a visitation from God. God told Moses to present himself to Him on the top of the mountain, where God had an appointment with him.

Part of the preparation for a revelation of God's glory is learning to come into God's presence, and presenting ourselves to Him. Just coming into His presence, not with a long prayer list, but just to be with Him. Moses went up the mountain and presented himself before the Lord and was there with the Lord for forty days and forty nights, and when he came down from the mountain, he did not know that the skin of his face shone from being in God's presence.

When Aaron and all the Israelites saw how Moses' face shone, they feared to come near him. Moses put a veil on his face so as to allay their fears, but whenever he went into God's presence, he took the veil off.

As we present ourselves to the Lord and consciously enter into His presence and enjoy communion with Him, we too will experience and reflect His glory. In these days God's people are learning to enter into His presence, not with any agenda but just saying, "Lord here I am. I present myself to you."

A Revelation of Who God Is

After Moses had asked God to show him His glory and had presented himself to Him, then God began to reveal Himself to Moses (Exodus 33:19-23). God told Moses to stand in the cleft of the rock and He put His hand over him while His glory passed by. The glory of God filled the atmosphere. After He had passed by, God took his hand away, so that Moses could only see Him from the back. God then began to speak to Moses and showed him what He was like.

> And the Lord passed before him and proclaimed, "The LORD, the Lord God, merciful and gracious, longsuffering and abounding in goodness and truth. Keeping mercy for thousands, forgiving iniquity and transgression and sin, by no means clearing the guilty, visiting the iniquity of the fathers upon the children, and the childrens' children, to the third and to the fourth generation." (Exodus 34:6,7)

30

Eleven Statements About God

When God revealed His glory to Moses, He made eleven statements about Himself, and each statement was a revelation of His glory.

One: **The LORD!** The LORD (capital letters) means Jehovah. The self-existent, the eternal One.

Two: **The LORD God!** The word God, is El, which means the One with strength and the One Who is mighty. As God passed by Moses, He wanted him to understand how mighty and how powerful He was.

Three: **Merciful!** One day God was angry with the children of Israel and He said to Moses, "Moses, I'm tired of these people, they are so rebellious and they have given me so much trouble, I'm going to wipe them out." And Moses said, "God, do You remember that You said that You were merciful? God I'm asking You to be merciful to these people." Because of His mercy, God spared their lives.

God is merciful and His mercy is available to us today. No matter what we might have done in the past, there is no sin that has gone so deep that the blood of Jesus cannot reach it.

> *If we confess our sins, He is faithful and just to forgive us our sins and to cleanse us from all unrighteousness.*
>
> (1 John 1:9)

The apostle Paul said that he was a harsh and wicked man, but he obtained mercy.

Four: **Gracious!** God is a gracious God and He wants us to experience His grace. He promises that His grace is sufficient for us, no matter what we might be going through. What is grace? Grace is God's unmerited favour towards us.

> **G** – God's
> **R** – Riches
> **A** – at
> **C** – Christ's
> **E** – Expense

Through the blood of Jesus and the finished work on the cross, God has made available to us all the grace that we need.

> *For out of His fullness (abundance) we all received – all had a share and we were supplied with – one grace after another and spiritual blessing upon spiritual blessing and even favour upon favour and gift heaped upon gift.*
>
> (John 1:16 Amplified)

Five: **Longsuffering!** The Apostle Peter reminds us that He is longsuffering, extraordinarily patient towards us not desiring that any should perish. God waits and waits and waits for people to be born again into the family of God.

> *The Lord does not delay and be tardy or slow about what He promises, according to some people's conception of slowness. But He is long-suffering (extraordinarily patient) toward you, not desiring that any should perish, but that all should turn to repentance.*
>
> (2 Peter 3:9 Amplified)

God is very patient with us, His children, and although He cannot tolerate sin, He patiently works in our lives to bring us to a place of repentance.

> *He has not dealt with us according to our sins, nor punished us according to our iniquities. For as the heavens are high above the earth, so great is His mercy toward those who fear Him.*
>
> (Psalm 103:10, 11)

Six: **Abundant in goodness!** God is not spiteful but He is abundant in goodness. He sends rain on the just and on the unjust and He daily loads us with benefits. The Bible reminds us that the earth is full of the goodness of the Lord. (Psalm 33:5) The prophet Nahum could also testify of His goodness.

> *The Lord is good, a strength and stronghold in the day of trouble; He knows, recognises, has knowledge of and understands those who take refuge and trust in Him.*
>
> (Nahum 1:7 Amplified)

Seven: **Abundant in truth!** The Hebrew word for truth is stability. God is abundant in stability. In certainty you can rest and guarantee yourself in God Who is abundant in truth. He is unchanging and His word can be depended upon.

> *God is not a man, that He should lie, nor a son of man that He should repent. Has He said, and will He not do it? Or has He spoken and will He not make it good .*
>
> (Numbers 23:19)

Eight: **Keeping mercy for thousands!** God keeps mercy for thousands of people, not just one or two. God has a bank full of mercy and over and over again, without us even being aware of it, He showers us with His mercy. David the Psalmist had an understanding of the extent of God's mercy.

> *For as the heaven is high above the earth, so great is His mercy toward them that fear Him.* (Psalm 103:11)

Nine: **Forgiving iniquity, transgression and sin!** Here we notice three words used to describe sin. **Iniquity** means perversity, **transgression** means revolt and **sin** means offence. God wants to forgive people who repent of their sin, whether it be in the form of perversity, revolt or any offense. The Bible reminds us that when God forgives our sins, He casts all our sins into the depths of the sea and He remembers them no more. He not only forgives, but He also releases us from the penalty of sin, which is everlasting damnation.

> *For the wages of sin is death, but the gift of God is eternal life in Christ Jesus our Lord.* (Romans 6:23)

Ten: **Who will in no wise clear the guilty!** God is merciful, but if we do not repent, He cannot show us His mercy, because He is also just and righteous. Mercy is conditional on our repenting of our sins. If we are guilty of sin and do not repent, He will not clear our guilt away.

Some people are involved in secret sins and if they wilfully choose to continue in them, they bring themselves under God's curse. God will in no way wipe our sin under the carpet. If you stand guilty before God right now, that cannot be changed by the mercy of God, unless you repent. The Bible reminds us that whoever confesses his sins shall prosper, but those who cover their sins shall not prosper. The Lord is merciful, but at the same time He is just and righteous.

Eleven: **Visiting the iniquity of the fathers upon the children and upon the children's children to the third and fourth generation!** There's no doubt about it that people will wilfully fall into sin and because of that, a curse will come upon them and be passed down to their family to the third and fourth generation. The ramifications of sin in a person's life does not only affect that person, but it affects their children and their children's children. Let us determine not to be responsible for bringing a curse on the future generations of our family. Praise the Lord, that that curse can be broken in the name of Jesus. If you sense that there is a curse on your family, call in a Spirit-filled Christian counsellor to agree with you and to break any family curses that may be on you and your family. Because of God's mercy, in the powerful name of Jesus, every curse can be broken and the enemy's power over you and your family will be rendered null and void.

Summary

These eleven statements that God spoke to Moses about Himself, gave him a clear portrait of Who God is and what He is like, and with this revelation of God, Moses had actually experienced God's many faceted-glory.

The first two statements speak of the fact that God is **mighty.** The next seven describe for us that God is **merciful.** The last two speak of the fact that God is **righteous.** Most people have only read the last two statements about God, and from that they have concluded that God is an angry and unfair God, who is standing with one hand on his hip and a rod in the other, ready to beat us at the first opportunity. The image of God that we have in our minds has been so distorted by the lies of the devil, that it has left us with a warped and twisted view of God. We need to ask God to reveal to us who He really is and begin to experience the tender, loving, Father-heart of God.

As we look at this incident in Moses' life, it's possible that God said to Moses, "Moses, I've been waiting and longing for somebody who would want to meet with Me and see My glory. Moses, this is what I am like, I am merciful, I am mighty, I am longsuffering, BUT I'm still righteous and just and I cannot tolerate sin. Moses, the good news is that you do not have to live in sin, but as you follow me with all your heart I will shower you with My mercy and grace and will help you to overcome sin. I will be longsuffering towards you and you will experience My abundant goodness and truth. As you experience these things Moses, you will be seeing My glory, and remember that I delight to show you My glory."

2.2 Experiencing God's Glory

God desires that all of His children should know the joy of experiencing His glory. Experiencing the glory of God is a breakthrough into the presence of God and an experiencing of God's character as portrayed through His mercy, grace, abundant love, truth, justice and many other virtues.

Experiencing the glory of God is far deeper than a mere rational, intellectual experience with God! It is meeting with God Himself. It is having a manifestation of God's presence! It is Spirit-to-spirit communication. God's Spirit communicating with our spirit and bringing us life and revelation from God.

Here's a man who has his quiet time, and he says, "Lord speak to me". As he opens the pages of scripture, God the Holy Spirit begins to speak to him and Jesus becomes so real to him that he is overwhelmed with the presence of God. What has actually happened is that God has manifested His presence to him and He has experienced God's glory.

From the scriptures we see that God longs to manifest Himself to us.

He who has My commandments and keeps them, it is he who

loves Me. And he who loves Me will be loved by My Father, **and I will love him and manifest Myself to him**.

(John 14:21)

This is having the New Testament equivalent of what Moses experienced in Exodus chapter thirty-three and thirty-four, when Moses asked God to show him His glory.

The question arises therefore, How many of us have seen the glory of God? Some of us have seen the first glimpses of the glory of God but there's so much more of His glory that we need to see.

The children of Israel saw the glory of God come down on Mount Sinai like a devouring fire.

> *Now the glory of the Lord rested on Mount Sinai... The sight of the glory of the Lord was like a consuming fire on the top of the mountain in the eyes of the children of Israel.*
>
> (Exodus 24:16, 17)

The Israelites also saw the glory of God come down on the tabernacle.

> *Then the cloud covered the tabernacle of meeting and the glory of the Lord filled the tabernacle.* (Exodus 40:34)

They also saw and experienced God's glory, when Solomon dedicated the house of the Lord. The glory of the Lord was so awesome and powerful, that the priests could not enter the house of the Lord.

> *When Solomon had finished praying, the fire came down from Heaven and consumed the burnt offering and the sacrifices, and the* **glory of the Lord** *filled the house. The priests could not enter the house of the Lord, because the* **glory of the Lord** *had filled the Lord's house. And when all the people of Israel saw how the fire came down and the* **glory of the Lord** *upon the house, they bowed with their faces upon the pavement, and worshiped and praised the Lord saying, For He is good, for His mercy and loving-*

kindness endure forever.   (2 Chronicles 7:1-3 Amplified)

Ezekiel saw the glory of the Lord. The Bible records for us how Ezekiel fell on his face when he saw the glory of God.

> *So I arose and went out into the plain and behold, the **glory of the Lord** stood there, like the glory which I saw by the River Chebar; and I fell on my face.*   (Ezekiel 3:23)

The shepherds saw the glory of God at the birth of Jesus, when the angel of the Lord appeared to to them.

> *And behold an angel of the Lord stood before them, and the **glory of the Lord** shone around them, and they were greatly afraid.*   (Luke 2:9)

Stephen saw the glory of God shortly before he was stoned to death.

> *But he, being full of the Holy Spirit, gazed into heaven and saw the **glory of God**, and Jesus standing at the right hand of God.*   (Acts 7:55)

We can see His glory

The heavens declare God's glory and every time you look up into the sky and see a beautiful sunrise or a sunset or look up at the stars, you are seeing the glory of God.

> *The heavens declare the **glory of God** and the firmament shows and proclaims His handiwork.*
>   (Psalm 19:1 Amplified)

As children of God we have the privilege on earth of seeing God's glory.

> *But we all, with unveiled face, beholding as in a mirror the glory of the Lord, are being transformed into the same image*

37

from glory to glory, just as by the Spirit of the Lord.

(2 Corinthians 3:18)

God allows us to experience His glory in small amounts. His glory is so enormous that our frail human bodies cannot handle the full extent of it. One day, when we see Jesus and receive our glorified bodies, will we be able to experience the glory of God in all its fullness. Charles G. Finney encountered a dynamic experience with God as he was waiting on God for more of His fullness. So great was the awesomeness of God's presence and His glory, that Finney had to ask God to stay His hand of blessing, because the weight of God's glory was too great for his human body to handle.

God's Glory is Revealed to Us Through Jesus

The God Who met with Moses, has revealed Himself to us through somebody that came to this earth and was born as a baby in Bethlehem and His name is JESUS. If we want to see God's glory, it will happen as we take a good long look at His Son Jesus Christ, Who said that He has come to give us life and to give it more abundantly.

And the Word (Jesus) was made flesh and dwelt among us, and we beheld His glory, the glory as of the only begotten of the Father, full of grace and truth. No one has seen God at any time. The only begotten Son, who is in the bosom of the Father, He has declared (revealed) Him. (John 1:14,18)

A Prophetic Word

God spoke to us through a prophetic word and said, "If you want to see My glory, look at My Son. In the Old Testament He was covered. In the New Testament He is come and we behold Him as with a veil that has been taken away from our faces. As we by faith approach the throne of grace, and draw near to Him and look into the face of the Son of glory, we will see billows of love flowing out towards us, love being poured into our spirits. As we look into His eyes, we will see forgiveness. We will sense His power flowing effortlessly and endlessly in and through us. Get close enough to look into His eyes, and let His love enrapture you, and let your soul be diffused with joy in His presence." Behold the glory of My Son!

The Holy Spirit Reveals God's Glory to Us

The Holy Spirit is the One Who makes God's glory and His presence a reality to us. Through the indwelling Holy Spirit we can have a foretaste of the blissful things to come because He is the guarantee of our inheritance, the deposit or down payment on our eternal heritage.

> *The Spirit is the guarantee of our inheritance – the first fruit, the pledge and foretaste, the down payment on our heritage – in anticipation of its full redemption and our acquiring complete possession of it, to the praise of His glory.*
>
> (Ephesians 1:14 Amplified)

Therefore, the more you want of God, the more you need the Holy Spirit.

> *Do not get drunk with wine, but ever be filled and stimulated with the Holy Spirit.* (Ephesians 5:18 Amplified)

The Holy Spirit needs to be welcomed as the senior partner in our lives. As we listen to and obey His gentle promptings He will unfold to us more and more of the glory of God, so that we will be able to say, "My eyes have seen the glory of the Lord."

Experiencing God's Glory through His Presence

Perhaps you ask the question, how can I as an individual, experience God's presence? There are several practical steps you can take, that will help you to experience the presence of God.

39

Become Quiet

In order for us to experience the reality of God's presence it is very important that we should learn to quieten our hearts, to put aside distracting thoughts and focus the eyes of our heart on Jesus.

> *Be still and know that I Am God.* (Psalm 46:10)

Sometimes we find it difficult to become still before God, but meditating on a Bible verse, like this one from Jeremiah, can help to quiet your spirit.

> *I have loved you with an everlasting love; therefore with loving-kindness I have drawn you.* (Jeremiah 31:3)

Spend time reflecting on the content of it. As you begin to meditate on God's unconditional love for you personally, your heart will become quiet and your spiritual senses will be awakened to the sense of God presence.

Turn Inwards

Once you have become still, turn your attention inwards towards your spirit.

> *...For indeed, the kingdom of God is within you.* (Luke 17:21)

St Augustine once said that he had lost much time in the beginning of his Christian experience, by trying to find the Lord outwardly, through outward circumstances, rather than turning inwardly toward his Spirit where Jesus dwells.

In order for us to experience God's presence and hear His voice, we have to learn to turn inwards towards our spirit, for it is there that we will find Him.

> *It is not in heaven, that you should say, Who will ascend into heaven for us and bring it to us that we may hear it and do it? Nor is it beyond the sea, that you should say, who will go over the sea for us and bring it to us that we may hear it and*

do it? But the word is very near you, in your mouth and in your heart, that you may do it. (Deuteronomy 30:12-14)

Turning inwards towards our spirit, is an art that we need to cultivate. We are so accustomed to operating on the rational level, that to begin to operate on the spiritual level is something we find difficult to do. The Bible encourages us to look more at the invisible things than the visible.

Look not to the things that are seen, but to the things that are unseen; for the things that are visible are temporal, brief and fleeting, but the things that are invisible are deathless and everlasting. (2 Corinthians 4:18 Amplified)

As we become quiet before God and turn inwards towards our spirit, without any agenda, simply to come into His presence, it opens the way for God to come and manifest Himself to us.

Enjoy His Presence

God longs for us to enjoy His presence. It is true to say that we are always in God's presence, but we only become aware of it as we take time to consciously draw near to Him. Once you become aware of His presence, linger there. You do not necessarily have to say anything, just keep looking at Him. If your mind starts to wander, refocus the eyes of your heart on to Jesus and tell Him that you love Him. As you do this your soul will be enraptured with joy and you will be nourished and strengthened in your inner man.

David the Psalmist, spoke about waiting on the Lord and encouraging himself in the Lord.

I have set the Lord continually before me, because He is at my right hand, I shall not be moved. (Psalm 16:8)

Imagine the Lord before you for a moment. There are several ways in which you can do this. Picture the Lord Jesus walking on the water towards you on the boat, or picture Him walking towards you on the seashore in Galilee. Try and focus in on the

41

Lord and see yourself alone with Him. As you look into His eyes, begin to enjoy His presence. You do not need to say anything except focus the eyes of your heart on to Him Picture Him looking directly into your eyes. Jesus Himself said that He would come and would manifest Himself to us, so expect Him to do that. Look at Him with the eyes of your heart and endeavour to hold your heart in His presence. After a while gently tell Him that you love Him and continue to stay in His presence for as long as possible. David had a passion for God's presence.

> *One thing have I desired of the Lord, that will I seek after, inquire for and insistently require, that I may dwell in the house of the Lord, in **His presence**, all the days of my life, to behold and gaze upon the beauty, the sweet attractiveness and the delightful loveliness of the Lord.*
>
> (Psalm 27:4 Amplified)

> *You will enrapture me diffusing my soul with joy, with and in **Your presence**.*   (Acts 2:28 Amplified)

Listen to His Voice

Once you have lingered in God's presence for a while, ask Him to speak to you and listen to His still small voice or look for a God-given picture. God's voice is often light and gentle and if you do not listen carefully, you can easily miss it. God's voice is sensed as a spontaneous idea that drops into your mind. Your own thoughts are analytical. You reason them out. Thoughts from God are spontaneous.

Record what He Says

When God speaks to you or shows you something, record what He says to you, so as not to forget the essence of what God has said. Sometimes it is very encouraging to go back and read what God said to you in a given situation.

Respond

Once God has spoken to you, then respond to His voice.

Obedience is the key to an ongoing relationship with Him.

Experiencing the reality of God's presence is not difficult. Simply becoming quiet and turning inwards towards your spirit where God dwells, is the key. Experiencing His glory is found in His presence. If we stay humbly at the feet of the Lord and passionately pursue His presence, God will be able to entrust us with more of His glory.

2.3 Changing From Glory to Glory

God's ultimate plan for us is that we should become like Jesus and change from glory to glory. Meeting Jesus as our personal Lord and Saviour, is the beginning of the greatest adventure of our lives. It is not a one-time experience, but it is the introduction to a whole new way of life. Being a Christian is a life of progress, in which we not only get to know more about the Lord but we become more and more like Him. Our relationship with the Lord never ends because there is always more of God that we can learn about and experience and we will never be able to say that we have arrived!

People Who do not Know the Lord are Blind about the Truth of God

Some people are blinded to the truth of God's word, in spite of the fact that they read the Bible. Until they have an encounter with Jesus and invite Him into their lives as their personal Saviour and Lord, they are blinded. However, when they meet with Jesus, their blindness is removed.

> *But their minds were blinded, for until this day the same veil remains unlifted in the reading of the Old Testament, because the veil is taken away in Christ. Nevertheless when one turns to the Lord, the veil is taken away.*
>
> (2 Corinthians 3:14,16)

Many Christians have been blinded by the devil to all that God has got in store for them, and have experienced very little of the abundant life that the Bible speaks about in John 10:10. Not only does God want us to accept Jesus as our personal Saviour and Lord, but He wants us to develop an ongoing, in-depth relationship with Himself. He desires that the eyes of our hearts be opened, so that we may see all the wonderful things that are available to us in Christ.

> *By having the eyes of your heart flooded with light, so that you can know and understand the hope to which He has called you and how rich is His glorious inheritance in the saints. And so that you know and understand what is the immeasurable and unlimited and surpassing greatness of His power in and for us who believe.*
>
> (Ephesians 1:18,19 Amplified)

Experiencing the Glory of the Lord Transforms Us

It is encounter with God's glory that transforms us into the likeness of Jesus.

> *And all of us, as with unveiled face, because we continued to behold (in the Word of God) as in a miror **the glory of the Lord,** are constantly being transfigured into His very own image in ever increasing splendor and from one degree of glory to another; for this comes from the Lord, Who is the Spirit.* (2 Corinthians 3:18 Amplified)

Transformation is a metamorphosis. Being changed into God's likeness is progressive. Little by little God is transforming us into His likeness. As we continue to behold, as in a mirror, the glory of the Lord, we are being transformed into His very own image, from one degree of glory to another. Every time we press into God's presence and experience intimacy with Jesus, we encounter His glory and change a little more into His likeness. The more you soak up God's presence, the more time we spend with the Lord, the greater the metamorphosis that takes place in us!

God's ultimate purpose with us is that we should become more and more like Jesus! We are not to seek to become like Billy

Graham or some other world-renowned figure, but we are to seek to become like the Lord Jesus Christ and this will not happen overnight, but will take place gradually. The face of Moses was transformed by his meeting with the Lord on the mountain!

A man from the Cape in South Africa was touched by the glory of God in a meeting that he was attending. He lay on the floor and began to shake and he thought he was going to fall apart. He did not know what was happening to him, because he was not even converted. The man then began to shout out and cry, "I must be born again, I must be born again." He got born again that night and that was the beginning of the transformation process in his life. Some may ask: "Can the glory of God be manifested to an unconverted person? Yes it can. It happened to Saul on the road to Damascus.

A certain pastor in South Africa was touched by the glory of God in a meeting where the Spirit of God was moving. He was literally flung out of his seat and lay on the floor in front of the stage and then began to roll up the stairs of the stage and then down again. The glory of God was all over him and he was stunned by the experience, unable to fully explain what had actually happened, except to say that he was dramatically touched by God that day and the transformation process in his life was propelled into action.

As God pours out His Holy Spirit on you, you may fall down under the power of God, but not be transformed. You may laugh or cry and not be transformed, you may become drunk with the new wine and still not be transformed. You may have many wonderful manifestations, which are just aids to help us get through to God and still not be transformed, but the change comes when we encounter Jesus as a living reality. It is looking into the face of Jesus and experiencing what John 14:21 speaks about as a reality in our lives. Personal encounter with the living God is what transforms us into His image.

The Ongoing Work of the Holy Spirit in Us

Experiencing the glory of God and being transformed into His image, is the ongoing work of the Holy Spirit in our lives. The

Holy Spirit is the One who removes our blindness, by firstly introducing us to Jesus, and then revealing more of Jesus to us. As the Holy Spirit takes us deeper and deeper into a life of intimacy with Jesus, He removes the blind spots, which are often philosophical interpretations of scripture that have no foundation whatsoever.

As we give the Holy Spirit full right of way in our lives and choose to make Him the senior partner, He will transform us into the likeness of Jesus and change us from one degree of glory to another. Just imagine what could happen in our cities, countries, continents and the world, if we were all transformed into the likeness of Jesus.

A New Liberty

The Holy Spirit brings us into a new liberty in God.

> *Now the Lord is the Spirit; and where the Spirit of the Lord is, there is liberty.* (2 Corinthians 3:17)

A great Baptist preacher once said that from the Greek structure of that verse, it would be correct to say that where the Spirit is LORD, where the Spirit is in control, there is liberty. Where the Spirit of God does not move, then everything works like clock-work. Where the Holy Spirit is allowed to move, there is a new liberty. People have liberty to raise their hands, to dance, to pray for the sick, to operate in the gifts of the Spirit. For most of us that liberty has gone so far and no further, but the Holy Spirit is removing the blind spots and leading us into a greater liberty than we have ever known before.

Yielding to the Control of the Holy Spirit

Yielding ourselves to the control of the Holy Spirit is the key to inheriting all the glorious things that God has planned for us in this life. Obedience to the gentle promptings of the Holy Spirit, brings us into glorious liberty.

*But now we are discharged from the Law and have
terminated all intercourse with it, having died to what once
restrained and held us captive. So now we serve not under
obedience to the old code of written regulations, but under
obedience **to the promptings of the Spirit** in newness of life.*
(Romans 7:6 Amplified)

Let's determine to keep on yielding to the control of the Holy
Spirit in our lives, so that He can bring us into a new liberty and
change us from glory to glory.

The Glory That We Must Give Him

It is important that we should give God the glory for all the
wonderful things that He has done and is busy doing. God alone
deserves praise and glory for He is the perfect One. He will not
share His glory with man.

Whenever God has used a person or a church, and they have
taken a shred of glory, tragedy has struck. God says, "My glory
will I not give to another". Under no circumstances will He give
His glory to another, because it belongs to Him. He must have the
pre-eminence in all things.

*I am the Lord; that is My name, and my glory will I not give
to another.* (Isaiah 42:8)

Devastating Results

Taking God's glory for ourselves, can result in devastation. The
story of Herod comes as a warning to us.

*And upon a set day Herod, arrayed in royal apparel, sat
upon his throne, and made an oration unto them. And the
people gave a shout saying, "It is the voice of a god and not
a man!" And immediately the angel of the Lord smote him,
because he gave not God the glory: and he was eaten of
worms, and gave up the ghost.* (Acts 12:21-23)

Herod's death was a Divine judgement on him, for receiving homage as a god. He was willing to receive worship, that was due to God alone and God's judgement fell on him. Let us remain humble before God, always recognizing that He is Lord.

2.4 Conclusion

The glory of God is you and I experiencing all that God has got for us. The glory of God can be revealed to us in several different ways, but ultimately it is encountering the presence of the living God personallly, that counts.

God longs to meet with us and the moment we choose to draw near to God, He draws near to us.

> *My beloved Shepherd said to me, "O my dove, while you are here in the seclusion of the clefts in the solid rock... let me see your face, let me hear your voice; for your voice is sweet and your face is lovely."* (Song of Solomon 2:14 Amplified)

Let us not settle for an impersonal relationship with Jesus, but determine to develop an ongoing, intimate relationship with Him, so that He can unfold more of His glory to us. The more of His glory we experience, the more we will be transformed into His likeness.

Prayer

Show me Your glory O God! Holy Spirit come and fill me now as I yield to Your control. Reveal Jesus to me as a reality. Come fire of God and transform me more and more into His likeness.

If you have enjoyed this book and would like to help us to send a copy of it and many other titles to needy pastors in the **Third World**, please write for further information or send your gift to:

> **Sovereign World Trust, P.O. Box 777, Tonbridge, Kent TN11 0ZS, United Kingdom**

or to the **'Sovereign World'** distributor in your country.